DRAWING ROBOTS AND ALIENS

with SCOOBY-DOO!

by Steve Korté
illustrated by Scott Jeralds

CAPSTONE PRESS
a capstone imprint

Published by Capstone Press, an imprint of Capstone.
1710 Roe Crest Drive
North Mankato, Minnesota 56003
capstonepub.com

Library of Congress Cataloging-in-Publication Data
Names: Korté, Steven, author. | Jeralds, Scott, illustrator.
Title: Drawing robots and aliens with Scooby-Doo! / by Steve Korté ; illustrated by Scott Jeralds.
Description: North Mankato, Minnesota : Capstone Press, [2022] | Series: Drawing fun with Scooby-Doo! | Includes bibliographical references. | Audience: Ages 8–11 | Audience: Grades 4–6 | Summary: "Uncover the clues you need to draw Scooby-Doo's most popular robots and aliens! With step-by-step instructions, you'll sketch Charlie the Funland Robot, the Nuclear Alien, the Star Creature, and so much more! Best of all, drawing these classic Scooby characters has never been more fun and easy!"—Provided by publisher.
Identifiers: LCCN 2021030536 | ISBN 9781663958877 (hardcover)
Subjects: LCSH: Robots in art--Juvenile literature. | Extraterrestrial beings in art—Juvenile literature. | Cartoon characters in art--Juvenile literature. | Drawing—Technique—Juvenile literature. | Scooby-Doo (Fictitious character)—Juvenile literature.
Classification: LCC NC1764.8.R63 K67 2022 | DDC 741.5/356--dc23
LC record available at https://lccn.loc.gov/2021030536

Editorial Credits
Christopher Harbo, Editor; Tracy Davies, Designer;
Katy LaVigne, Pre-Media Specialist

Design Elements
Shutterstock: BNP Design Studio, Ori Artiste, sidmay

TABLE OF CONTENTS

LET'S DRAW ROBOTS AND ALIENS WITH SCOOBY-DOO!

It's past midnight in Crystal Cove. Strange events have been happening in a deserted field at the edge of town. There have been reports of UFOs—unidentified flying objects—that look like spaceships. Others have reported seeing dangerous robots on the loose. Fortunately, one brave team is on the prowl. The five members of the Mystery Inc. gang rush down the road inside their brightly colored Mystery Machine van. Fred Jones is behind the wheel. Fellow team members Velma Dinkley and Daphne Blake are sitting beside him. And at the back of the van, Shaggy Rogers and his canine pal, Scooby-Doo, peer nervously out the van's windows.

CLANK! CLANK! The sound of metallic footsteps fills the air. Is it a robot on the rampage?

ZOOOOM! A bright light washes over the van. Is it a rocket ship from another planet?

"Zoinks!" cries Shaggy.

"Roinks!" agrees Scooby.

Fred hits the brakes and jumps out of the Mystery Machine. Velma and Daphne are right behind him. Scooby-Doo and Shaggy both groan with dismay.

"Come on, gang," calls out Fred. "It looks like we have a mystery to solve!"

Over the years, Mystery Inc. has battled many mechanical monsters and out-of-this-world aliens. Let's see how many of these terrifying trouble-makers you can draw!

WHAT YOU'LL NEED

You are about to draw a collection of rampaging robots and otherworldly aliens! But you'll need some basic tools to draw these creepy creatures. Gather the following supplies before starting your art.

paper

You can get special drawing paper from art supply and hobby stores. But any type of blank, unlined paper will work fine.

pencils

Drawings should always be done in pencil first. Even the pros use them. If you make a mistake, it'll be easy to erase and redo it. Keep plenty of these essential drawing tools on hand.

pencil sharpener

To make clean lines, you need to keep your pencils sharp. Get a good pencil sharpener. You'll use it a lot.

erasers

As you draw, you're sure to make mistakes. Erasers give artists the power to turn back time and undo those mistakes. Get some high-quality rubber or kneaded erasers. They'll last a lot longer than pencil erasers.

black marker pens

When your drawing is ready, trace over the final lines with a black marker pen. The black lines will help make your characters stand out on the page.

colored pens and markers

Ready to finish your masterpiece? Bring your characters to life and give them some color with colored pencils or markers.

Charlie the Funland Robot

1

Look out! Here comes a menacing metal creature, known as Charlie the Funland Robot. Originally created to help run the Funland Amusement Park, someone has sabotaged the robot's circuits. Charlie is now programmed to destroy Mystery Inc.!

2

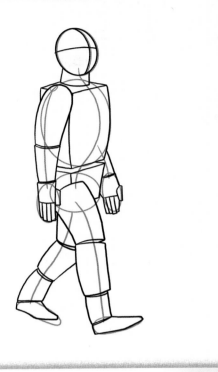

3

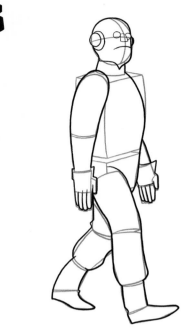

4

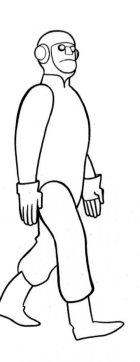

5

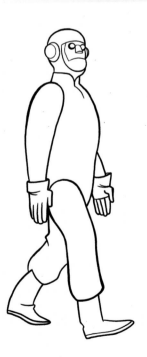

Snow Beast

A trip to the North Pole turns terrifying when the gang meets the Snow Beast. This giant robot looks like a furry dinosaur with razor-sharp claws and fangs. Weighing more than two tons, the Snow Beast towers over Scooby and the gang. Can they figure out a way to make this creature go extinct?

1

2

3

4

5

Spooky Space Kook

Is the Spooky Space Kook an alien or a ghost? Or both? This massive creature in a blue spacesuit has a skull for a head and two eerie, red glowing eyes. When the gang meets this freaky monster near an abandoned airfield, Scooby-Doo is too scared to even finish his oversized Jaw-Dropper Sandwich.

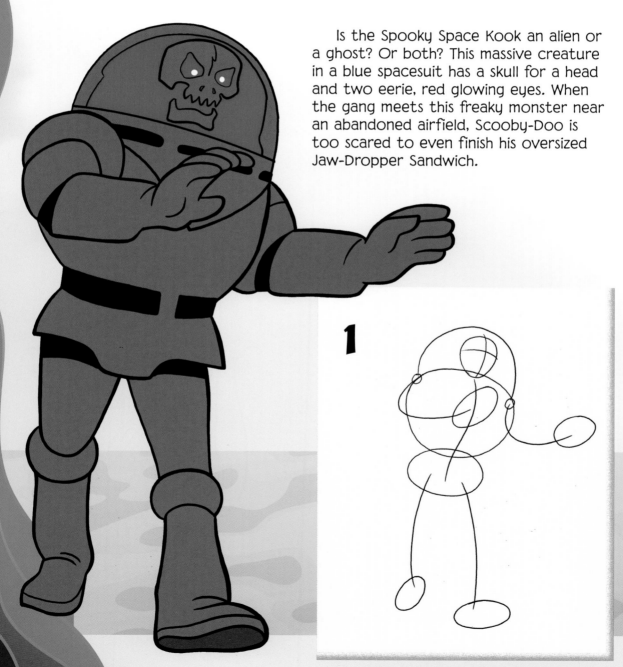

1

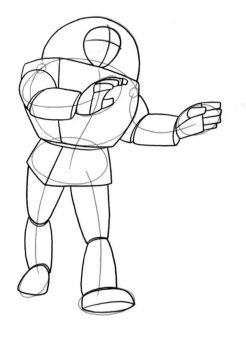

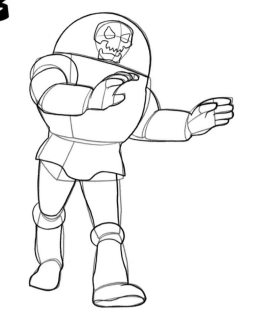

Future Monster

A time machine experiment goes horribly wrong when Professor Simon Grady accidentally brings a giant beast from 5,000 years in the future back to the present day. The Future Monster has huge bug-eyes and pointy claws and fangs. The creature is half-man and half-insect, and it is 100 percent creepy!

1

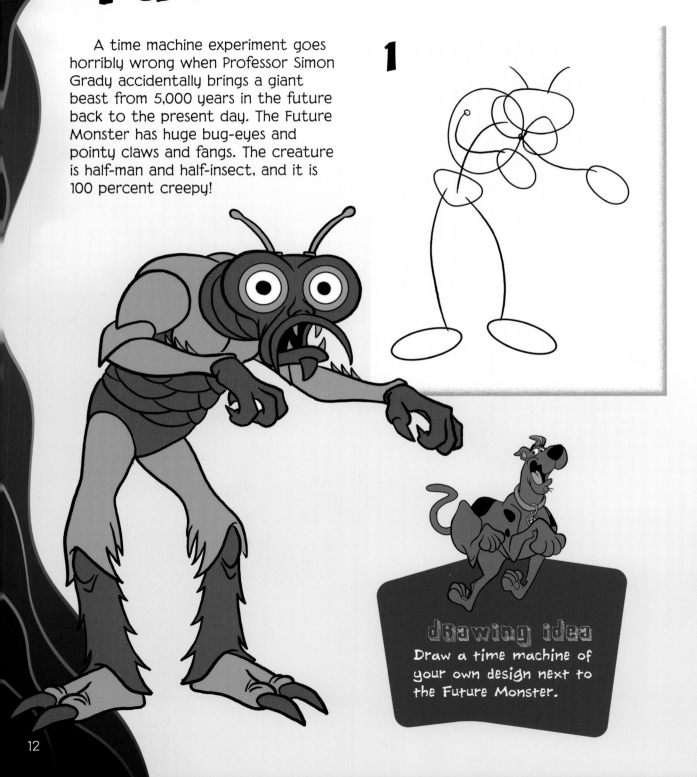

dRawing idea

Draw a time machine of your own design next to the Future Monster.

2

3

4

5

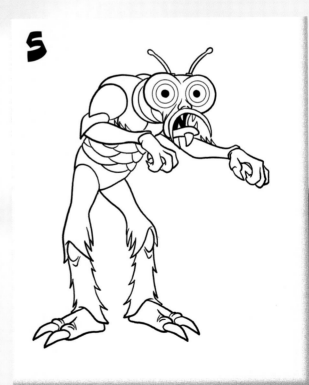

Evil Alien

Ruh-roh! Scooby-Doo, Shaggy, and Scrappy-Doo take a trip in a spaceship and meet this metal menace on another world. Even worse, the trio soon learns that this creature has the word "Evil" in its name. "Like, that's not a good sign," says Shaggy.

1

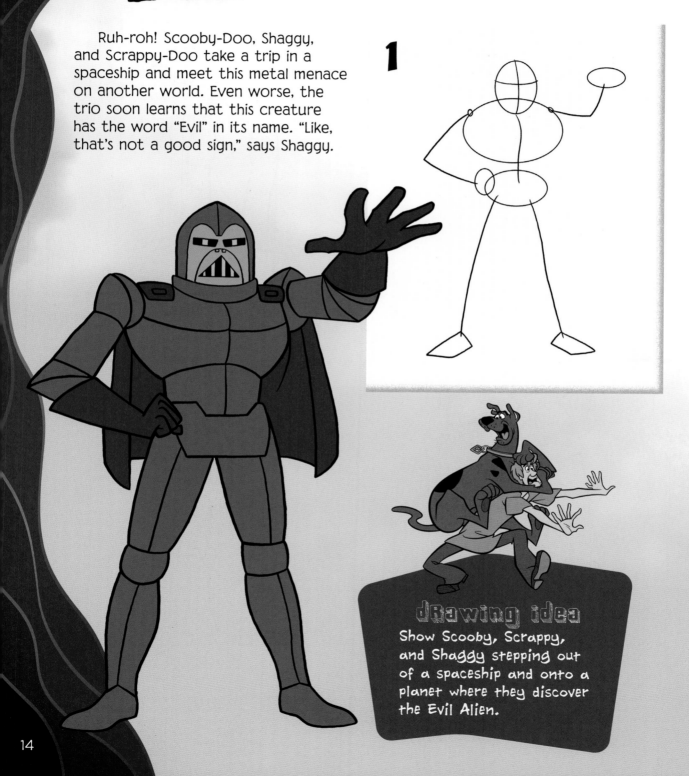

dRawing idea

Show Scooby, Scrappy, and Shaggy stepping out of a spaceship and onto a planet where they discover the Evil Alien.

2

3

4

5

Rawhide Red

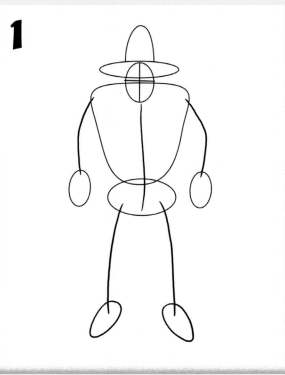

1

A trip to a Wild West theme park called Robot Ranch gets a little too wild for Scooby and the gang. They meet up with the super-smart and super-dangerous Rawhide Red. Can the team figure out how to reprogram this risky robot?

2

3

4

5

Star Creature

There's trouble at Star Laboratory! A strange glowing creature shaped like a star is stealing secret codes from the lab's observatory telescope. "Zoinks!" says Shaggy, when he sees the Star Creature's sharp and very shiny claws.

1

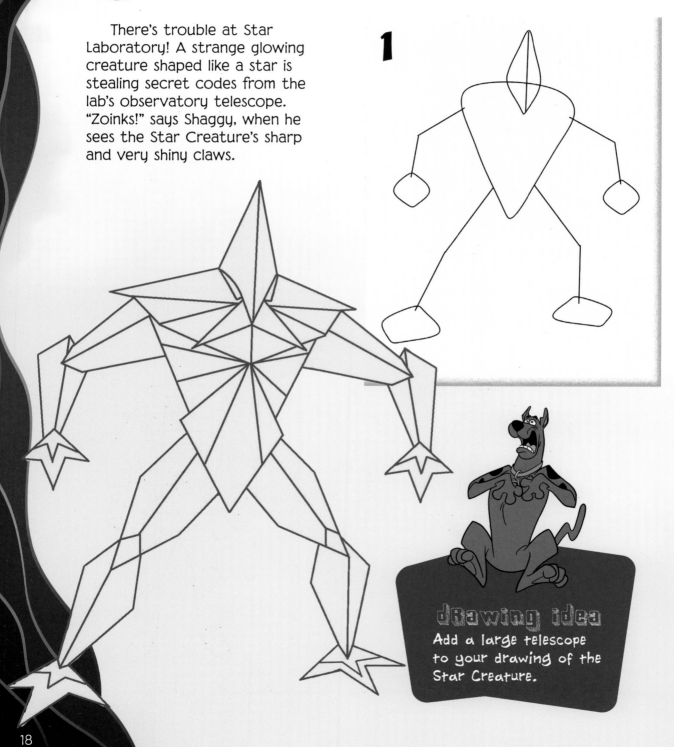

dRawing idea
Add a large telescope to your drawing of the Star Creature.

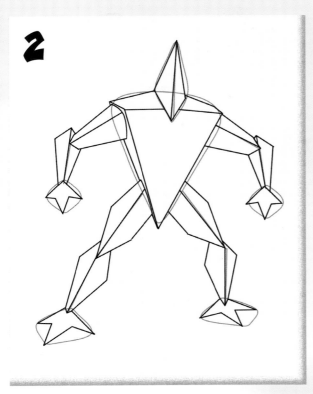

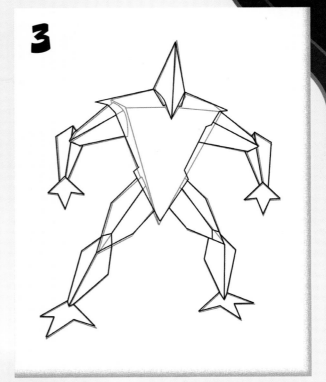

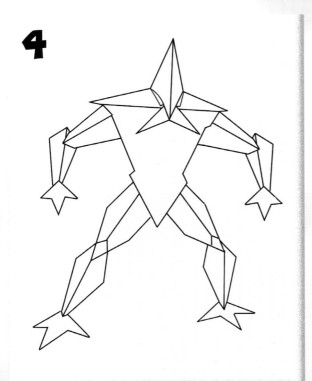

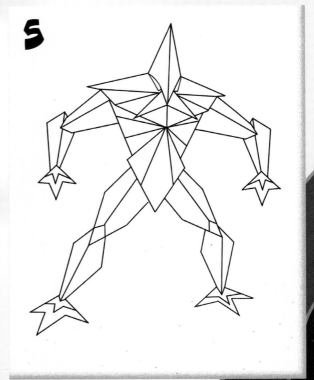

Mars Robot

BLAM! A rocket ship takes off for Mars with three accidental passengers—Scooby-Doo, Scrappy-Doo, and Shaggy! After landing on the Red Planet, the three encounter the Mars Robot. This metallic creature turns out to be a six-million-dollar research robot built on Earth!

1

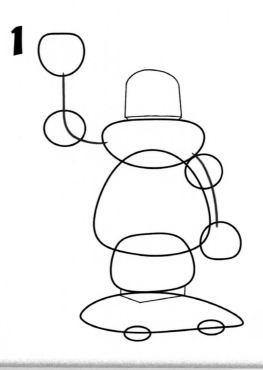

dRawing idea

Add a Martian background to your drawing. Then draw Scooby, Scrappy, and Shaggy too!

Monster Mouse

1

The massive Monster Mouse is ten times larger than the Mystery Inc. gang. It also has a bigger appetite than Shaggy and Scooby-Doo combined! Is this humongous rodent a scientific experiment gone wrong or an evildoer's mechanical robot? It's up to Scooby and the gang to figure it out.

dRawing idea

The next time you draw Monster Mouse, show it grabbing Scooby-Doo with one of its giant paws.

Nuclear Alien

When a billion dollars goes missing from a nuclear research laboratory, all clues point to a glowing, radioactive space alien as the robber! "It looks like we have a mystery to solve," declares Fred, as the team tracks down the creepy-looking creature.

1

dRawing idea

Show Daphne bravely confronting the Nuclear Alien. Be sure to draw a glow around the creature.

24

2

3

4

5

Body-Snatcher Alien

1

"Ruh-roh!" Scooby cries when he first sees the Body-Snatcher Alien. This creepy creature has green skin, a cone-shaped head, and many legs. It has traveled to Earth with a triple-trouble plan to create clones of Scooby, Scrappy, and Shaggy!

dRawing idea

Show Scooby, Scrappy, and Shaggy running away from the evil Body-Snatcher Alien.

Escaping Charlie the Funland Robot

"Like, get us out of here!" yells Shaggy as a fun day at the amusement park turns frightfully freaky! He and Scooby are on the run from a rampaging robot. Will they get chased down by Charlie or escape the mechanical menace?

1

2

3

4

5

MORE DRAWING FUN!

Bird, Benjamin. *Monster Doodles with Scooby-Doo!* North Mankato, MN: Capstone Press, 2017.

Harbo, Christopher. *10-Minute Drawing Projects.* North Mankato, MN: Capstone Press, 2020.

Sautter, Aaron. *How to Draw the Joker, Lex Luthor, and Other DC Super-Villains.* North Mankato, MN: Capstone Press, 2015.

MORE SCOOBY-DOO FUN!

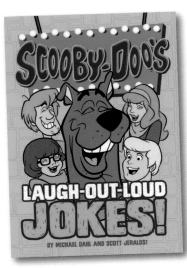

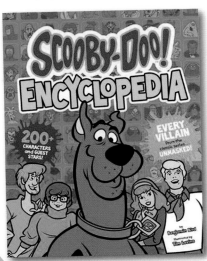